Rest.
FOR THE SOUL

30-DAY DEVOTIONAL

Shawanda Williams

Cocoon to Wings
PUBLISHING

REST FOR THE SOUL
Copyright © 2020 Shawanda Williams

All rights reserved. This book or any portion thereof may not be reproduced, distributed, or transmitted in any form or by any means, including photocopying, recording, or other electronic or mechanical methods, without the express written permission of the publisher except in the case of brief quotations embodied in critical reviews and certain other noncommercial uses permitted by copyright law. For permissions requests, write to the publisher, addressed "Attention: Permissions Coordinator," at the address below.

Printed in the United States of America
ISBN: 978-1-7347494-0-3 (Paperback)

Library of Congress Control Number: 2020907193

Published by Cocoon to Wings Publishing
7810 Gall Blvd, #311
Zephyrhills, FL 33541
www.StephanieOutten.com
(813) 906-WING (9464)

Scriptures marked NLT are taken from the HOLY BIBLE NEW LIVING TRANSLATION (NLT): Scriptures taken from the HOLY BIBLE, NEW LIVING TRANSLATION, Copyright ©1996, 2000, 2002, 2003 by Holman Bible Publishers, Nashville Tennesee. All rights reserved.

Scriptures marked NIV are taken from the NEW INTERNATIONAL VERSION (NIV): Scripture taken from THE HOLY BIBLE, NEW INTERNATIONAL VERSION® Copyright ©1973, 1978, 1984, 2011 by Biblica, Inc.™ Used by permission of Zondervan

The Holy Bible, New King James Version® Copyright ©1982 by Thomas Nelson, Inc. All rights reserved.

Book design by Ereka Thomas Designs

Rest
FOR THE SOUL

CONTENTS

Week One
We Can't Have True Rest Apart from God's Word — 2

Week Two
Rest is Healing for Your Soul — 20

Week Three
The Path of Rest Leads to Wholeness — 36

Week Four
Rest In The Pace of God — 52

Week Five
Rest is a Place You Live — 68

Week Six
Rest in His Promises — 84

FOREWORD

Rest... A small word that unfolds enormous possibilities. As a person who wears many hats, husband, father, mentor, spiritual advisor & pastor, rest is a crucial part of my life. There is value in putting things on "pause" and allowing yourself to be restored. Rest is spiritual, physical, mental and emotional attention to oneself. It is something, I believe, we all long for but many have missed out because of not understanding the many facets of it.

Shawanda has caught the heart of "Rest" and placed key aspects in this book. I've known her for over 30 years and seen her grow in grace, wisdom and strength. This book is part of her journey and revelation she received from the Lord. She is a member of our church and a dynamic part of our ministerial leadership team.

I pray you invest in yourself and make this book part of your library of "Spiritual Self-Care & Maturity." As you begin this devotional, you will discover how to take the necessary steps in finding "Rest for the Soul."

Tony Peterson
Senior Pastor- Co Founder
Every Walk of Life Ministries

*To my pastors, Tony and Angela Peterson,
and my kids, Shamari, Maurice, and Marcus.
Thank you for loving me through and walking
with me on my journey to rest.*

Dear Son & Daughter of God,

Let me first begin by telling you how excited and honored I am to share with you this treasure found in God's word! When applied daily, it will bring richness to your home, your workplace, your everyday living, but most importantly, to your soul! It's **Rest! Yes, REST!!**

Through this 30-day devotional, we will debunk what culture defines as rest and renew our minds with God's word to understand what rest is, why it is essential in the life of a believer, and how we can live it daily! Through the week, you are given a devotional, and on the weekends, we will journey through the story where Jesus calms the storm in Mark 4, one verse at a time.

My favorite part of this devotional is the daily meditation scripture, journal entry, and song you are given under *"My Hiding Place."* In your intimate time with your Father, you will write down the scripture for the week and the words that come alive to you every day for five days. A new daily meditation scripture will be given each week. I believe God is going to open your heart and speak something new and enlightening to you each day!

My prayer for you is that this devotional will soften your heart to receive the revelation of rest. I pray those hidden places in you that may have been disturbed are exposed and healed through this God-given Rest! I declare that when you find rest, you will find wholeness, a new perspective, and a purpose that will catapult you into God's design and destiny for your life!

Blessings and Favor to you on this transformational journey,

~Shawanda

WE CAN'T HAVE TRUE REST APART FROM GOD'S WORD

Week One

Day 1

To Rest is to Be Silent.

One morning, sadly, like most mornings, I was frantically rushing to get the kids out of the house in time for school. After sliding the last PB&J into a ziplock bag, I looked down at my phone to check the time, and the usual anxiety began to tighten in my chest. I had two minutes to leave, or I would have to suffer *the car line.*

Just as I was tossing a jelly-stained knife into the dishwasher, I heard a whisper in my spirit. *"Rest."* I disregarded the small voice and yelled out to the kids, "Did you brush your teeth?... Did you brush your hair?... Did you put your homework in your backpack?" Not too long after, I hear the voice again. *"Rest."* Knowing now that the Holy Spirit was gently nudging me to rest, I responded, "How can I rest now when I have to get the kids to school?" I went on about my day, but the word *rest* lingered in my thoughts. Why was the Holy Spirit telling me to rest, and why at the busiest time of my day? Soon I would discover that rest was for the soul, not just the body.

Somehow we have made rest to be something inconvenient or recreational rather than necessary and daily. Rest is not supposed to disturb you or disrupt your rhythm. It is the silence to the disturbances within your soul so that you can live in the rhythm of an abundant life. Anxiety is a disturbance within the soul. So, the Holy Spirit wasn't telling me to stop what I was doing. Instead, He was speaking to the loud anxiety within me and telling it ***to be silent.***

What needs ***to be silent*** within your soul? Fear can become so loud that you are unable to hear God whisper, *"I'm with you. I'm your hiding place. I promise never to leave you."* Or negative self-talk can drown out the voice of the Holy Spirit saying, "*I love you. You are fearfully and wonderfully made. You have a purpose.*"

As we begin this journey of rest, I believe the Holy Spirit will whisper to the need in your soul all along the way. ***Be silent*** in Him and hear what He is speaking to you. Healing and true rest awaits you!

Rest (damam): To be silent

We Can't Have True Rest Apart from God's Word

Day 1

"My Hiding Place"

"Rest in the Lord, and wait patiently for Him;
Do not fret because of him who prospers in his way,
Because of the man who brings wicked schemes to pass."

PSALMS 37:7 (NKJV)

Write the scripture above:

....
....
....

Word(s) that come alive for me from this scripture:

....
....

What is God saying to me through these words?

....
....
....
....
....

🎧 **SONG FOR YOU**   WORD OF GOD SPEAK BY MERCYME

We Can't Have True Rest Apart from God's Word

Day 2

To Rest is to Be Still.

Yesterday we learned that rest is just as much for the soul as it is for the body. It is an internal silence. Rest also means **to be still.** Sometimes our souls can become so loud in its emotions that we can't hear or remember the Word of God, and so we respond out of fret, rage, guilt, offense, fear, you name it. These emotions are what I like to call *disturbances* to the soul.

A disturbance is the interruption of a settled and peaceful condition. Our souls naturally crave to be in a peaceful condition...to be at rest...*to be in stillness.* The condition of our souls is reflected on the outside of us. I find that those who have a hard time keeping physically still, whether it's not being able to sit still in their own home or not being able to remain at one job for long, also have disturbances on the inside that are not still. What is not still within us will eventually move us out of alignment of God's will for our life.

Let's take a part of Elijah's story, for example. Elijah, God's prophet, killed a lot of false prophets to destroy their false religions. King Ahab told his wife, Jezebel, all that Elijah had done. So, she threatened to kill Elijah, and Elijah ran. Her threat caused a disturbance of fear, and because he did not *still the fear*, the fear moved him to run. I love that in 1 Kings 19, God spoke to Elijah in a *still*, small voice and asked him why he was in the place he was. Not the physical place, but this disturbed place in his soul that moved his physical place.

Maybe it's not fear, but weariness that needs to be stilled within your soul. We can become weary when we are following God's plan and remaining attentive to His word but don't see the change we've been expecting. I understand this place, and so does Paul. That is why he included himself when he said, "And let us not grow weary while doing good, for in due season we shall reap if we do not lose heart." Galatians 6:9 (NKJV). We are given commands in scripture not to fret and not grow weary because we have the power to still these emotions, and if we don't, it can move us out of place. Let's *still* these disturbed places in our souls by being still in who God is and what He is saying. Hear the still, small voice of our Father, for He is the Comforter of our souls.

Rest (damam): To be still

We Can't Have True Rest Apart from God's Word

Day 2

"My Hiding Place"

> "Rest in the Lord, and wait patiently for Him;
> Do not fret because of him who prospers in his way,
> Because of the man who brings wicked schemes to pass."
>
> **PSALMS 37:7 (NKJV)**

Write the scripture above:

....
....
....

Word(s) that come alive for me from this scripture:

....
....

What is God saying to me through these words?

....
....
....
....

🎧 **SONG FOR YOU**   BE STILL BY TRAVIS GREENE

We Can't Have True Rest Apart from God's Word

Day 3

To Rest is to Die.

How can we die and still physically live? According to Psalms 37:7, it is fret that has ***to die***. Fret is to be angry, constantly worry or be anxious, or weariness. David makes a command not to fret because he knows it can happen. Constantly worrying or being anxious is a distraction from resting in the Lord. The scripture that comes to mind when I see the word *die* is in 1 Corinthians 15:31, where Paul writes that he dies daily! Rest is not an overnight, one-time deal. Just as sure as you wake up again, so can worry and fear. Therefore, this is an intentional lifetime practice and process.

We can be physically alive while our soul is dying from anxiety because we allow it to consume us instead of putting it on the altar. But how do we kill it? The answer is in Psalms 37:7. Rest **in the Lord.** The part of us that frets can only die in who we know the Lord to be! We know the Lord by spending time in His word and building an intimate relationship with Him. It is hard to rest and trust in someone you do not know or have not experienced life with. Our Father wants you to know Him and experience His broad love for you. "Then Christ will make his home in your hearts as you trust in him. Your roots will grow down into God's love and keep you strong. And may you have the power to understand, as all God's people should, how wide, how long, how high, and how deep his love is." Ephesians 3:17-18 (NLT). All God's people should know His great love because it is when we know who the Lord is that we then understand who we really are and the authority we walk in!

When we feel anxiety rising, we have the power to arrest anxiety and hold it captive to the word! I have learned to kill anxiety on the onset by speaking out loud, *"I cast all of my cares on you, God, right now, because your word says that you care for me. I have nothing to worry about because your word promises you will never leave me. I will not be anxious, but instead, I ask that you give me strength and grace in this moment."* After I have done this, I find that an ease comes over my soul. Anxiety has ***to die*** to the Word of God! When we rest in Him, we are resting in what the Word says about Him and who we have learned Him to be for ourselves. Therefore, we can't have **true rest apart from God's word!**

Rest (damam): To die

We Can't Have True Rest Apart from God's Word

Day 3

"My Hiding Place"

> "Rest in the Lord, and wait patiently for Him;
> Do not fret because of him who prospers in his way,
> Because of the man who brings wicked schemes to pass."

PSALMS 37:7 (NKJV)

Write the scripture above:

....

....

....

Word(s) that come alive for me from this scripture:

....

....

What is God saying to me through these words?

....

....

....

....

....

🎧 **SONG FOR YOU** GRACEFULLY BROKEN BY TASHA COBBS LEONARD

We Can't Have True Rest Apart from God's Word

Day 4

To Rest is to Quiet Self.

There are times we need to go to a quiet place to think, hear, and sense the presence of God. My closet, my shower, and my car are a few of my regulars. I find that when I am in quiet, I am also able to hear and sense where I am.

When we **quiet self,** we allow ourselves to come to an honest place in our soul**.** The hustle and bustle of life can keep the most toxic parts of us hidden if we continue in that rhythm. God called Adam out of this rhythm of hiding when he asked him in the Garden of Eden, "Where are you?" This question was more so for Adam to locate himself, to reason within his soul that he was no longer in the naked and unashamed place God created him to be. They were in a rhythm and place of rest, and the enemy didn't like it. The enemy comes to kill, steal, and destroy that rest by separating us from the Word of God. It's the same trick he used then, and it's the same trick he uses now.

When we are separated from His word, shame and a slew of other things can come on us and cause us to live in unrest. So, we must make regular time to **quiet ourselves** in the presence of God. It is then we can hear what's loud and out of rhythm, and we can call it out! We can speak to shame and tell it to go because God sent His Son to nail shame to the cross. The enemy will have to back up, and shame will be quiet!

Where are you? If you have to, find a quiet place so you can get to that honest place. It's time to come out of hiding! God is calling you out of that old rhythm you've been in too long. He is bringing you back to the place where you were created to create, to thrive, to live naked and unashamed!

Rest (damam): Quiet Self

We Can't Have True Rest Apart from God's Word

Day 4

"My Hiding Place"

> "Rest in the Lord, and wait patiently for Him;
> Do not fret because of him who prospers in his way,
> Because of the man who brings wicked schemes to pass."
>
> **PSALMS 37:7 (NKJV)**

Write the scripture above:

....

....

....

Word(s) that come alive for me from this scripture:

....

....

What is God saying to me through these words?

....

....

....

....

🎧 **SONG FOR YOU** — HOLY SPIRIT BY JESUS CULTURE

We Can't Have True Rest Apart from God's Word

Day 5

To Rest is to Grow Dumb.

As we end this first week on the last definition of rest, I want to use the first verse you will study this weekend from Mark 4:35 to give you a further understanding of what it means to grow dumb. Jesus tells the disciples, "Let's go to the other side of the lake." Jesus doesn't give much detail on when they will get to the other side, why they are going to the other side, or what they might encounter in the middle of them going to the other side. He gives a simple, one-sentence instruction for the disciples to follow.

We live in such an age where we have unlimited access to information in seconds. There are things my thirteen-year-old daughter knows that she teaches me! While having knowledge and understanding is essential, it can also be a hindrance if that is what we find rest in.

The Holy Spirit gives us instruction and leading in part, not all at once. John 16:13 (NKJV) says, "However, when He, the Spirit of truth, has come, He will guide you into all truth; for He will not speak on His own authority but whatever He hears He will speak; and He will tell you things to come." Don't overthink it or run two steps ahead of God when He has only given you one step. Often I have to reel my thoughts back in when I notice I'm going too far into what could or what might be. Don't let dreaming take you out of a place of rest where you have clasped onto an idea and not the word He gave you. Our smarts or guessing won't get us there, so we have to be intentional in learning to rest in the one word He gives us.

Write the book, start the business, go back to school. **_Grow dumb_** in that word, because you don't know anything else but what He said. That is all you know and all you need to know at that time. This way, even if a storm comes to disturb what you know God told you, you are not wavered by what it looks like, because you never rested in the idea of what it had to look like. Instead, you found rest and anchored your soul in the one word He gave you. Therefore, you will be able to remain in the high winds of a storm and say boldly, "He said, 'Let's go to the other side,' so we are going to the other side!"

Rest (damam): Grow Dumb

We Can't Have True Rest Apart from God's Word

Day 5

"My Hiding Place"

"Rest in the Lord, and wait patiently for Him;
Do not fret because of him who prospers in his way,
Because of the man who brings wicked schemes to pass."

PSALMS 37:7 (NKJV)

Write the scripture above:

_____

_____

_____

Word(s) that come alive for me from this scripture:

_____

_____

What is God saying to me through these words?

_____

_____

_____

_____

🎧 **SONG FOR YOU**   EVERLASTING GOD (YOUR VERSION PREFERENCE)

We Can't Have True Rest Apart from God's Word

Verse for the Weekend:

> "As evening came, Jesus said to his disciples, "Let's cross to the other side of the lake."
>
> **MARK 4:35 (NLT)**

What stood out to me in the above verse?

Who or what is my Father leading me to cross over (grow past/mature in)?

Where in my life do I need to practice rest?

REST IS HEALING FOR YOUR SOUL

Week Two

Day 1

Come to Me.

Jesus says, *"Come to me."* It is a bold yet gentle invitation. He wants us. He wants you. No strings attached, just a promise that when we come to Him, He will give us rest. Our souls demand satisfaction, so who or what we decide to come to will either give our souls rest or a temporary substitute for it.

There are many substitutes we use to ease our souls, such as isolation; overconsumption of alcohol, drugs, or food; fornication; infidelity; validation from others; lashing out; shutting down; overcompensation in work, kids, or number of friends; runner (from places or people). My sister or brother, don't feel condemned if you find yourself resorting to any of these substitutes. God is still calling for you right now. He is meeting you right here at this well, where you are. "Whoever drinks of this water will thirst again, but whoever drinks of the water I shall give him will never thirst. But the water that I shall give him will become in him a fountain of water springing up into everlasting life." John 4: 13-14 (NKJV).

How do we drink this God-given water of rest for our soul? The Samaritan woman asked the same, and Jesus first had her to acknowledge what she was substituting to ease her thirsty soul, a soul that was living in un-rest. This is where we begin to enter **rest that is healing for our soul.** We have to come to an honest place of admission that our soul has been restless and thirsty and then identify what we have been coming to in order to satisfy it.

Over the next few days, let's walk this out together. Ask God to help you come to an honest place where you have been restless in your soul. Write down what you have been doing or using to ease this place. Then let's practice coming to God first and allow Him to give us something different, something better, something everlasting! He made us a promise that we will never thirst for those substitutes again!

Rest (anapauo): To cease from movement in order to recover strength

Rest is Healing for Your Soul

Day 1

"My Hiding Place"

> "Come to Me, all you who labor and are heavy burden,
> And I will give you rest. Take my yoke upon you
> And learn from Me, for I am gentle and lowly in heart,
> And you will find rest for your souls."
>
> **MATTHEW 11:28-29 (NKJV)**

Write the scripture above:

....
....
....
....

Word(s) that Come alive for me from this scripture:

....
....

What is God saying to me through these words?

....
....
....

🎧 **SONG FOR YOU** — NEVER RUN DRY BY CASEY J

Rest is Healing for Your Soul

Day 2

Your souls.

Our souls house the way we perceive, understand, feel, judge, and determine. In short, our souls are our perceiver, thinker, feeler, and chooser. Jesus gives us a promise that when we come to Him with our weariness, He will *refresh* the way we perceive, think, feel, and choose. The way we see ourselves determines the way we see life and others. The way we see life shapes our thoughts and feelings and leads to the way we respond. Our responses ultimately lead us to our destiny. So, for us to fulfill the destiny God designed for us, it begins with seeing ourselves properly through the grace lens of God. How do you view yourself? Who do you say that you are? God knows who you are and sees you for who He made you to be and not for what you do or feel!

I remember one day, in particular, I was talking to the Holy Spirit about my insecurities. I was weary and kept repeating that I was tired of being insecure. The Holy Spirit gently but firmly said, *"Stop saying you are insecure. You are not insecure."* At that moment, I realized I had been judging my identity on the way I felt, and because I saw myself this way, I responded to others with timidity. If I trace back my timid response, it will lead to an insecure perception of myself. God refreshed my soul and gave me the revelation that we are not what we feel! We are spirits that possess a soul and live in a body. "For God has not given us a spirit of fear and timidity, but of power, love, and self-discipline." 2 Timothy 1:7 (NLT).

We are not our souls; we just possess one. And you have the authority to align anything that is in your possession with the Word. Everything that God's Word says you are, you have to believe and speak even if your feelings are contrary to it. But this is also why God beckons you to come to Him to refresh *your souls*. He wants us to live an abundant life where we are not walking around, struggling between what we feel and who we are. His love and the renewal of our minds through His word will bridge this broken gap. What an amazing and loving Father we have!

So when you feel heavy or weary, take a moment to trace those feelings back to the perception of yourself. Allow God's word to heal and refresh you here. He wants rest to abide in the place you may perceive yourself to be insecure as it will set the trajectory of your destiny. Find refreshment in His word of who you are and watch how you align with what He predestined for you from the start!

Rest (anapauo): To refresh

Rest is Healing for Your Soul

Day 2

"My Hiding Place"

> "Come to Me, all you who labor and are heavy burden,
> And I will give you rest. Take my yoke upon you
> And learn from Me, for I am gentle and lowly in heart,
> And you will find rest for your souls."
>
> **MATTHEW 11:28-29 (NKJV)**

Write the scripture above:

_____
_____
_____
_____

Word(s) that Come alive for me from this scripture:

_____
_____

What is God saying to me through these words?

_____
_____
_____

🎧 **SONG FOR YOU** | I AM LOVED / THERE IS NOTHING BETTER BY MAVERICK CITY MUSIC

Rest is Healing for Your Soul

Day 3

My yoke.

Dear Father,

I come to you for your child that is reading this now. Lord, first, I want to say thank you. You are truly a good-good Father. A Father who cares about the soul of your child. Thank you for inviting us to come to you, to learn from you, to receive your rest you so freely give. Father, we are laying down every care and worry at your feet today. We choose to take your yoke instead. Your yoke is easy, light, and gentle. Anxiety will no longer have a grasp around our necks. Fear has to loose itself from our shoulders. Weariness must bow in your presence. Teach us how to lean into your strength daily. Father, our souls need you daily. We. Need. You. Nothing else will satisfy the quench in our souls than the rest your love brings. I pray we continue to free-fall into your loving arms, for the fullness of joy is there…freedom is there…peace is there…your rest is there. So we choose you. We choose your yoke. In Jesus' name, Amen.

Love,
   Your Child

Rest (anapauo): Take ease

Rest is Healing for Your Soul

Day 3

"My Hiding Place"

> "Come to Me, all you who labor and are heavy burden, And I will give you rest. Take my yoke upon you And learn from Me, for I am gentle and lowly in heart, And you will find rest for your souls."
>
> **MATTHEW 11:28-29 (NKJV)**

Write the scripture above:

....

....

....

....

Word(s) that Come alive for me from this scripture:

....

....

What is God saying to me through these words?

....

....

....

🎧 **SONG FOR YOU** — PSALM 42 BY TORI KELLY

Rest is Healing for Your Soul

Day 4

Take.

One evening my son came running into our living room, jumping up and down crying, "It hurts, it hurts!" I looked down at the finger he was holding out and noticed it was the same finger that had a splinter in it last week. I couldn't get the splinter out, so I decided to let it come out on its own. Well, that day, something must have touched that tender spot on his finger that wasn't completely healed and caused him pain. I tried to put an antibiotic ointment on it, but he refused to let me touch it, afraid I would cause him more pain. He was traumatized by the pain.

Soul trauma. Whether you are aware of it or not, some of us are walking around with a traumatized soul, afraid to be touched. Trauma is a deeply distressing or disturbing experience. I've recently learned that someone who has remained in a relationship where they have experienced infidelity for over five years is considered trauma. Trauma changes the mindset of a person. This experience now alters the way they view themselves. Maybe it wasn't infidelity for you. It could have been a sudden death. Or perhaps you were severely bullied as a child, molested, or grew up in an environment of an insecure or angry parent. Whatever the disturbance you may have experienced, if it has not been healed, your perspective of yourself is altered. Man has no cure for trauma; only therapy and medication are used to help individuals manage or numb the trauma.

Only God can heal a traumatized soul because He created the soul. My brothers and sisters, He is beckoning you to let him heal that tender part of you that is easily angered, defensive, or offended. He wants you to **take** His ointment by allowing Him to touch what has been deeply wounded. He is the balm for your soul! Yes, there will be temporary discomfort, but it's to get you to a place of true comfort, a place of rest for your soul!

Rest (anapauo): To keep quiet

Rest is Healing for Your Soul

Day 4

"My Hiding Place"

> "Come to Me, all you who labor and are heavy burden,
> And I will give you rest. Take my yoke upon you
> And learn from Me, for I am gentle and lowly in heart,
> And you will find rest for your souls."
>
> **MATTHEW 11:28-29 (NKJV)**

Write the scripture above:

....

....

....

....

Word(s) that Come alive for me from this scripture:

....

....

What is God saying to me through these words?

....

....

....

🎧 **SONG FOR YOU**   ALL I NEED BY BRIAN COURTNEY WILSON

Rest is Healing for Your Soul

Day 5

I will.

You can take God at His word. When He says He will do something, He will do it! He made a promise to heal and calm your soul *when* you come to Him. God wants all of you. He wants all of your heart, mind, and soul to be brought into His presence daily. When we love God with all of who we are, even the flawed parts of us that we prefer to keep hidden, we will begin to see ourselves as a child loved unconditionally by our Father. "Jesus said to him, 'You shall love the Lord your God with all your heart, with all your soul, and with all your mind.' This is the first and great commandment." Matthew 22:37-38 (NKJV).

Every time we come to God first and bring Him who we are and what we have at that moment, we are loving Him first. We are worshipping Him in spirit and in truth. This vertical transaction of love first begins with you and God so that then your horizontal love to others is infused with this Godly love. "And the second is like it: 'You shall love your neighbor as yourself.'" Matthew 22:39 (NKJV).

What if I told you that God not only wants to heal your soul through His love, but there is a domino effect attached to your healing where other souls will be healed too? On Day 1 of this week, we read about the Samaritan woman who came to Jesus with an empty bucket and an empty heart. Jesus gave her perspective on what her soul needed and the husbands she was using to satisfy it. The end of this transaction resulted in the Samaritan woman telling others about this man, and they also came to believe in Jesus for themselves. God says, "*I will* when you come. Now, will you come?" Will you bring Him your heart, your soul and your mind? Will you come so that He can fill that restless place with His love?

A commentary quote from Matthew Henry, nonconformist minister and author; *"Love is the rest and satisfaction of the soul; if we walk in this good old way, we shall find rest."*

Rest (anapauo): To keep of calm and patient expectation

Rest is Healing for Your Soul

Day 5

"My Hiding Place"

> "Come to Me, all you who labor and are heavy burden, And I will give you rest. Take my yoke upon you And learn from Me, for I am gentle and lowly in heart, And you will find rest for your souls."
>
> **MATTHEW 11:28-29 (NKJV)**

Write the scripture above:

....

....

....

....

Word(s) that Come alive for me from this scripture:

....

....

What is God saying to me through these words?

....

....

....

🎧 **SONG FOR YOU** MORE THAN ANYTHING BY NATALIE GRANT

Rest is Healing for Your Soul

Verse for the Weekend:

> "So they took Jesus in the boat and started out, leaving the crowds behind (although other boats followed)."
>
> **MARK 4:36 (NLT)**

What stood out to me in the above verse?

When following Jesus' way of rest, what do I need to leave behind?

Where are some physical places you can go to refresh/rest in God?

THE PATH OF REST LEADS TO WHOLENESS

Week Three

Day 1

Stop.

"Although we are feeling things all the time, if we never **stop** to be still, we can never identify and examine those feelings and what may be underneath," Toure Roberts, pastor and author, says in his book, *Wholeness.* He goes on to mention that this type of busyness that robs us of stillness puts us in a place where, instead of making life happen, we allow life to happen to us through unseen patterns. It's time to break the pattern and enter rest for your soul!

When was the last time you stopped to ask yourself, "Why do I feel this way?" Don't be afraid of what answer may lie beneath, as it may be a false truth about yourself that needs to be uprooted. We break the pattern by getting to the root of *why* we do what we do and feel the way we feel. And God will be right there with you, guiding you through it all. There is a version of you underneath these unseen patterns that God designed and needs to be discovered. He designed you in His image to be a creator, not a reactor! Just like the misplacement of the letter 'c' in creator changes the entire word. The misplacement of how we *see* ourselves changes the whole outcome of our lives. The way we perceive ourselves affects the way we see life, and the way we see life shapes our thoughts and feelings, which leads to the way we respond and ultimately impacts our destiny. The next time you feel a disturbance in your soul, whether it's anger, anxiety, fear, or shame, **STOP** and ask yourself, *Why am I feeling...?* Give God space to minister to you in this area and interrupt this pattern. God wants you whole and thriving! He wants you to enter a place of rest where you are creating the life you were always destined to live!

Perception > Thoughts > Feelings > Response > Destiny

Rest (margowa): A resting place

The Path of Rest Leads to Wholeness

Day 1

"My Hiding Place"

"This is what the Lord says: Stop at the crossroads and look around.
Ask for the old, godly way, and walk in it. Travel its path,
and you will find rest for your souls.
But you reply, 'No, that's not the road we want!'"

JEREMIAH 6:16 (NLT)

Write the scripture above:

....

....

....

....

Word(s) that come alive for me from this scripture:

....

....

What is God saying to me through these words?

....

....

....

🎧 **SONG FOR YOU**   WANTED BY DANNY GOKEY

The Path of Rest Leads to Wholeness

Day 2

Travel its path.

This. Is. A. Journey. The road to rest is not an easy, overnight, or comfortable ride. Somehow we have made salvation the one and only choice that matters as believers. Yes, it is the best decision a person can make for their lives, but it doesn't end there. We become clay on the Potter's wheel, where His loving hand cuts away dead things, molds the shape of our image into His Son, and refines us by fire. God is making you into His Masterpiece, and in the process, there are times you just want to get off and take the easier, less painful route.

I want to encourage you to continue to choose to ***travel the path*** God lays before you. Rest is worth the wait! God is more concerned about building our character and rooting our hope in Him rather than our comfort. "And not only that, but we also glory in tribulations, knowing that tribulation produces perseverance; and perseverance, character; and character, hope." Romans 5:3-4 (NKJV). He knows what it will take to cut insecurity from you so that you can walk in the security and comfort of Him. So, you may experience valley seasons in order for God to cut away at the part of you that likes to run from shadows. He wants to mold you into an unmovable and fearless believer who knows you are safe because of who you walk with!

My brothers and sisters, don't get off the path too early because of what it may feel like or doesn't feel like. Just because it's not comfortable, doesn't mean it's not God! Stay committed to where He has you. The rest area is up a mile! Wholeness is at your next exit!

Rest (margowa): A resting place

The Path of Rest Leads to Wholeness

Day 2

"My Hiding Place"

> "This is what the Lord says: Stop at the crossroads and look around. Ask for the old, godly way, and walk in it. Travel its path, and you will find rest for your souls. But you reply, 'No, that's not the road we want!'"
>
> **JEREMIAH 6:16 (NLT)**

Write the scripture above:

....

....

....

....

Word(s) that come alive for me from this scripture:

....

....

What is God saying to me through these words?

....

....

....

🎧 **SONG FOR YOU** — POTTER BY TAMELA MANN

The Path of Rest Leads to Wholeness

Day 3

You will.

Dear Son/Daughter,
   *When I created you, I knew what I had in mind for you, for your life. I knew what I wanted you to accomplish on this earth. I knew the skills and gifts to fashion you with so you could carry out the purpose I have for you. When I created you, I started from the end of you. Yes, you are fearfully and wonderfully made, and **you will** create fearfully and wonderfully things. Yes, you are more than a conqueror because **you will** not only defeat generational cycles, but **you will** live abundantly, and your family will call you blessed. **You will** find wholeness in Me. Nothing will be lacking, missing, or broken. I know the plans and good future I have for you, and **you will** see them all come to pass. I've seen the hurdles child, and I know it can look high at times, but I've seen that **you will** jump every one of them...some with tears, some with fears, but all with My strength. **You will** do all things through Me because I give you strength. It is My will to always be there and never leave you, to love you and never forsake you, to help you through it all. Because I will, **you will**.*

~Your Loving Father

Rest (margowa): A resting place

The Path of Rest Leads to Wholeness

Day 3

"My Hiding Place"

> "This is what the Lord says: Stop at the crossroads and look around. Ask for the old, godly way, and walk in it. Travel its path, and you will find rest for your souls. But you reply, 'No, that's not the road we want!'"
>
> **JEREMIAH 6:16 (NLT)**

Write the scripture above:

Word(s) that come alive for me from this scripture:

What is God saying to me through these words?

🎧 **SONG FOR YOU** SO WILL I BY HILLSONG WORSHIP

The Path of Rest Leads to Wholeness

Day 4

And look around.

The busyness and routine of our lives are thieves of the time we need to take to examine ourselves. Experts estimate that the mind thinks between 60,000 - 80,000 thoughts a day. That is a lot of thinking! Earlier, we learned that our perceptions of ourselves lead to thoughts, which leads to the way we feel. If we don't slow down ***and look around*** at the thoughts and feelings we have, we will miss blind spots that can cause crashes on the road to our destiny.

When we choose to take the path of rest, it can feel like we changed the gear down a notch. But slowing down to examine our thoughts and why we think what we think reveals the areas that are at unrest within us. You are no longer passing each day's experience with a grazed look, but intentionally looking around at your responses and feelings and then tracing it back to your perspective. As I have practiced this, I found myself uprooting a 17-year-old unforgiveness that I was unaware of because it had been in my blind spot.

God wants you to live a life that is free of disturbances, so much so that He sent His Son to die for it. "The thief does not come except to steal and to kill and to destroy. I have come that they may have life and that they may have it more abundantly." John 10:10 (NKJV). That life more abundantly is a life free from insecurities, unforgiveness, fear, and all the things that will hinder you from living the God-intended life. A life that is real, genuine, full, and vigorously devoted to Him!

So, look around and take **the path of Rest; it leads to Wholeness!**

Rest (margowa): A resting place

The Path of Rest Leads to Wholeness

Day 4

"My Hiding Place"

> "This is what the Lord says: Stop at the crossroads and look around. Ask for the old, godly way, and walk in it. Travel its path, and you will find rest for your souls. But you reply, 'No, that's not the road we want!'"

JEREMIAH 6:16 (NLT)

Write the scripture above:

....

....

....

....

Word(s) that come alive for me from this scripture:

....

....

What is God saying to me through these words?

....

....

....

🎧 **SONG FOR YOU**   GOD I LOOK TO YOU BY BETHANY WOHRLE

The Path of Rest Leads to Wholeness

Day 5

The crossroads.

Have you ever watched a show where someone is walking a long road and then comes up to a sign that has two opposite directions? The person can't tell at first which direction to take because both paths look similar, but they ultimately go with their instincts and make a choice. You have a choice! How you respond to life, it is a choice! The choice will always be between your way and God's way.

According to Jeremiah 6:16, the end of the godly path is rest. The Israelites knew what God promised them if they followed His path. Yet each time they were at *the crossroads* of hardship or the unknown, they chose the path they wanted. When we are cut off in traffic, we can find ourselves at a crossroads. When our discomfort pressures us to leave a job that God hasn't given us a release from, we can find ourselves at a crossroads. When your marriage is in shambles and God tells you to forgive your spouse, you can find yourself at a crossroads. So how do we press into God's path when we're at a crossroads?

"Jesus said to him, "I am the way, the truth, and the life. No one comes to the Father except through Me." John 14:6 (NKJV). Jesus' way of living should be the mirror to how we respond to life. We find Jesus at a crossroads when he's in prayer at the Garden of Gethsemane before allowing himself to be captured by those who wanted him killed. He asked the Father if he could deliver him from the suffering he would have to endure, but that God's will be done over his own will. One, we have to be honest with God and ourselves about what we want and how we feel. When you bring God your truth, you make room for Him to minister to that need in your soul. "Then an angel appeared to Him from heaven, strengthening Him." Luke 22:43 (NKJV). Two, give God space to tell you His will for you. Don't allow feelings to become so strong that you leave no opening for Him to guide you and give you wisdom. Initially, it may not be the path you want, but the destination to rest surely is!

Rest (margowa): A resting place

The Path of Rest Leads to Wholeness

Day 5

"My Hiding Place"

> "This is what the Lord says: Stop at the crossroads and look around. Ask for the old, godly way, and walk in it. Travel its path, and you will find rest for your souls. But you reply, 'No, that's not the road we want!'"
>
> **JEREMIAH 6:16 (NLT)**

Write the scripture above:

Word(s) that come alive for me from this scripture:

What is God saying to me through these words?

🎧 **SONG FOR YOU**   THE WAY BY PAT BARRETT

The Path of Rest Leads to Wholeness

Verse for the Weekend:

"But soon a fierce storm came up.
High waves were breaking into the boat,
and it began to fill with water."

MARK 4:37 (NLT)

What stood out to me in the above verse?

....

....

....

....

....

When high waves break into my life, what is my reply?

....

....

....

....

....

Where am I on this path to rest according to Jeremiah 6:16?

....

....

....

....

....

REST IN THE PACE OF GOD

Week Four

Day 1

Remember what it says.

When my kids were younger, I remember putting up a sign on their bathroom mirror, reminding them to brush their teeth and wash their face. Then they would come downstairs, and I would still ask, "Did you brush your teeth and wash your face?" Sometimes the answer was no because they would forget to look at the sign!

As we learned in Week 1, we can't have true rest apart from God's word, so as children of God, we must **remember what it says.** James 1:25 (NKJV) reads, "But he who looks into the perfect law of liberty and continues in it, and is not a forgetful hearer but a doer of the work, this one will be blessed in what he does." His Word is life, and we want to live the blessed life it promises us if we continue in it. To continue in it is to stay in the rhythm of remembering and doing God's word.

Let's take a closer look at James 1:25 again and the order of the words. It says when he looks, continues, is not forgetful, does, he will be! There is a consistent pace of looking at God's word, remembering it, and doing it before we can become it. Consistency is key to your God-ordained destiny! Maybe you have tried practicing rest and have been reading God's word for an internal breakthrough, but so far, you don't see a change. Well, here is the secret to change --continue in it! Don't stop looking, don't stop remembering, don't stop following His word!

The Word and a good heart are sure to yield good fruit. "The seed that fell on good soil represents those who truly hear and understand God's word and produce a harvest of thirty, sixty, or even a hundred times as much as had been planted!" Matthew 13:23

(NLT). You can only produce who you are! So, remember His Word with your heart. Don't focus so much on memorizing the letter of the law that you miss the spirit of the law. God never intended for us to be able to recite scriptures and not live them. He wants this word to become so much a part of you that it's just like knowing to brush your teeth and wash your face every day without forgetting!

Rest (katapausis): A resting place

Rest in the Pace of God

Day 1

"My Hiding Place"

"Remember what it says: "Today when you hear his voice, don't harden your hearts as Israel did when they rebelled."
So we see that because of their unbelief
they were not able to enter his rest."

HEBREWS 3:15, 19 (NLT)

Write the scripture above:

....

....

....

....

Word(s) that come alive for me from this scripture:

....

....

....

What is God saying to me through these words?

....

....

🎧 **SONG FOR YOU**   PROPHESY YOUR PROMISE BY BRYAN & KATIE TORWALT

Rest in the Pace of God

Day 2

Don't harden your hearts.

We are clay and the essence of who we are lies in our hearts. Our heart is like a room in the house of our soul. It's our passions, desires, affections, the way we perceive, think, feel, and choose. When we put our clay-like hearts into the hands of our Father with a posture of being shaped into what He desires for us, our passions become His passions, our desires are His desires, and the way we think aligns with His thoughts.

God is always molding and moving us into His design and destiny for us, but it takes a soft heart to bend to His will. A soft heart is one that is pliable and teachable. A hardened heart wants its own way, doesn't want to change, and refuses correction and discomfort.

What is the posture of your heart? This is a question you will have to ask yourself over and over again as you encounter challenging times. But I'm a witness that the hardness of life doesn't have to **harden your heart**. Divorce is painful, but it doesn't have to harden your heart from loving again. A tragic death can alter the way you look at life, but it doesn't have to harden your heart from living again. Bankruptcy can feel like a setback, but it doesn't have to harden your heart from believing you can be financially successful again. Know that you have the freedom and the power to choose your hearts' posture despite what difficulty comes your way.

"We now have this light shining in our hearts, but we ourselves are like fragile clay jars containing this great treasure. This makes it clear that our great power is from God, not from ourselves." 2 Corinthians 4:7 (NLT). On our own we are fragile clay, but when we rest our hearts in the treasure of the Holy Spirit to guide and comfort us, we access a great power from God that keeps us from becoming hard, defeated and destroyed. "We are pressed on every side by troubles, but we are not crushed. We are perplexed, but not driven to despair. We are hunted down, but never abandoned by God. We get knocked down, but we are not destroyed." 2 Corinthians 4:8-9 (NLT). **Don't harden your heart.** Instead, remain pliable and soft in the hands of your Father. When you rest, He'll work.

Rest (katapausis): A putting to rest

Rest in the Pace of God

Day 2

"My Hiding Place"

> "Remember what it says: "Today when you hear his voice, don't harden your hearts as Israel did when they rebelled."
> So we see that because of their unbelief
> they were not able to enter his rest."
>
> **HEBREWS 3:15, 19 (NLT)**

Write the scripture above:

....

....

....

....

....

Word(s) that come alive for me from this scripture:

....

....

What is God saying to me through these words?

....

....

🎧 **SONG FOR YOU**   TELL YOUR HEART TO BEAT AGAIN BY DANNY GOKEY

Rest in the Pace of God

Day 3

Today.

I want to challenge you *today* to create time for solitude and silence. It is easy to get into a pace of busyness and hurry that slowing down our life feels abnormal. We're restless *today* because of tomorrow. We're constantly thinking about what's next or what has to be done. We have goals, meetings, ministry, careers, family, and social media that pulls at us and keeps us moving and thinking. We feel compelled to say yes and guilty for saying no. Your body and mind need rest!

God rested after creating for six days, not because he was tired, but because he was creating rest for us. You have permission to rest because you are to do what you see your Father do! "And God blessed the seventh day and declared it holy, because it was the day when he rested from all his work of creation." Genesis 2:3 (NLT). It is holy to rest! The word holy means sanctified, to be set apart, to be kept sacred. Rest (shabath) used in this scripture means to cease and to celebrate. God set aside sacred time to cease from what he was doing and to celebrate what he had done.

In your solitude *today*, set yourself apart from noise, distractions, and put to rest the thoughts of tomorrow. Celebrate what you have accomplished over this past week or yesterday. Celebrate the fact that you finally got to wash that load of laundry. Celebrate living *today*! Play a worship song, lay prostrate before God, and celebrate who He is and His faithfulness to you. Rest is no longer contained to one day out of the week. It is who we are and how we live. Intentionally take steps to make rest your new normal!

Rest (katapausis): A putting to rest

Rest in the Pace of God

Day 3

"My Hiding Place"

> "Remember what it says: "Today when you hear his voice, don't harden your hearts as Israel did when they rebelled." So we see that because of their unbelief they were not able to enter his rest."
>
> **HEBREWS 3:15, 19 (NLT)**

Write the scripture above:

....

....

....

....

Word(s) that come alive for me from this scripture:

....

....

What is God saying to me through these words?

....

....

....

🎧 SONG FOR YOU — REST IN YOU BY HILLSONG

Rest in the Pace of God

Day 4

His rest.

Rest is given by God; it was created by Him. There are other manipulated forms of rest we can try to ease our souls with, but ***His rest*** is a calming of the winds within us.

Let's take the Israelites, for example. Because they were under condemnation for 400 years, they developed a disturbance, a storm, within themselves that the Lord wanted to calm. Their perception of themselves was disturbed by the strong disapproval of the Egyptians. So the Lord took the Israelites down a longer path to the Promise Land to change this mindset. But instead of the Israelites believing in the God who rescued them, they believed Egypt could ease the fear of the unknown in their hearts. "...whom our fathers would not obey, but rejected. And in their hearts they turned back to Egypt," Acts 7:39 (NKJV). Maybe this path you're on with God feels long and slow. You're believing Him for His promises, but it seems like it's taking forever to manifest. God is faithful and loves you so much that He knows who you need to become to enjoy His promises. He is not withholding anything from you that you need now.

Rest
    in
        the
            pace of God.

God wants your heart to remain turned to Him. He is calming the winds of fear within you and teaching you to trust Him instead of what you've always known. Trust the path and the process He has you on, and you will surely enter ***His rest!***

Rest (katapausis): A calming of the winds

Rest in the Pace of God

Day 4

"My Hiding Place"

> "Remember what it says: "Today when you hear his voice, don't harden your hearts as Israel did when they rebelled."
> So we see that because of their unbelief
> they were not able to enter his rest."
>
> **HEBREWS 3:15, 19 (NLT)**

Write the scripture above:

Word(s) that come alive for me from this scripture:

What is God saying to me through these words?

🎧 **SONG FOR YOU**   EYE OF THE STORM BY RYAN STEVENSON

Rest in the Pace of God

Day 5

Hear His voice.

Dear Father,

*Thank you for another day that you have made. I choose to be glad and rejoice in today. For you have seen today from beginning to end, so Father, I bend my ear and heart to you to be led by your voice. Guide me, O'Lord, in the way I interact with people, in the decisions I make, and the words that I should or should not say. My heart is softened to receive your word because I believe you. I trust you. Your word promises that when I **hear your voice** and do what you say, I will be able to enter your rest. I speak your rest over my family, over my mind, and over every hidden area in my soul that longs for you. Lord, I want every part of my life to be engulfed by your rest. Give me discernment to know your voice from mine and the enemy. Your voice is all that matters. Your voice is what created me. Your voice is what saved me. Your voice is what calms the winds within me. I will wait to **hear your voice.** Today, I choose your voice over all the others. I love you, Father. In Jesus' name, Amen.*

Love,
~Your Child

Rest (katapausis): A calming of the winds

Rest in the Pace of God

Day 5

"My Hiding Place"

> "Remember what it says: "Today when you hear his voice, don't harden your hearts as Israel did when they rebelled."
> So we see that because of their unbelief
> they were not able to enter his rest."
>
> **HEBREWS 3:15, 19 (NLT)**

Write the scripture above:

Word(s) that come alive for me from this scripture:

What is God saying to me through these words?

🎧 **SONG FOR YOU**   NOTHING ELSE BY CODY CARNES

Rest in the Pace of God

Verse for the Weekend:

"Jesus was sleeping at the back of the boat with his head on a cushion. The disciples woke him up, shouting, 'Teacher, don't you care that we're going to drown?'"

MARK 4:38 (NLT)

What stood out to me in the above verse?

....
....
....
....

Who am I growing to be most like in the eye of a storm? Jesus or the disciples?

....
....
....
....

When what I see doesn't line up with God's word, what is one scripture my heart turns to?

....
....
....
....
....

REST
IS A
PLACE
YOU LIVE

Week Five

Day 1

My place.

I love the comfort of my home. Farmhouse table, chandelier, scented candles, decorative pillows, and soft throws. This is ***my place***. It's warm, cozy, and inviting. There's nothing like coming home from a long day at work and lighting my candles, wrapping myself in a warm blanket, and flopping in my spot on the couch. I like being comfortable and comfortable likes me, and I believe this is true for most of us. However, we can become comfortable in our own toxic thoughts, in unhealthy eating habits, or even in abusive relationships.

Toxic, unhealthy, and *abusive* are not warm, cozy, and comfortable words, yet how have our souls found a home in these places? I realized that it's not just the candles and pillows that make ***my place*** comfortable, it's because it is the place I come home to every day. I could visit a friend's house who had the same warm atmosphere and not feel the same comfort I feel in my own home.

Toxic thinking is a place we allow our souls to take residence in because we go there often. Going to a place of rest in God can feel like visiting a friend's house. It's uncomfortable at first because you are not used to resting in a place you've never been to. When we are uncomfortable, we feel unprotected and vulnerable to harm.

Our souls naturally want to be at rest and will try to grasp at anything to ease it. It wants to be comfortable. Your daily communion with Him in His Word, in prayer, and worship will help fight the compulsion to go back to what you once called home. Don't be like the Israelites and consistently turn away from the open door to God's place of rest because it's not comfortable. It will take some discomfort to get to His place of true comfort for your soul, but believe me, you will get there! Once you experience the comfort of God's place of rest, you will sing as David sang in Psalm 27:4 (NLT), "The one thing I ask of the Lord - the thing I seek most - is to live in the house of the Lord all the days of my life, delighting in the Lord's perfections and meditating in his Temple."

Rest (menuwchah): Comfortable

Rest is a Place You Live

Day 1

My Hiding Place

"For forty years I was angry with them, and I said,
'They are a people whose hearts
turn away from me. They refuse to do what I tell them.'
So in my anger I took an oath: 'They will never enter my place of rest.'"

PSALMS 95:10-11 (NLT)

Write the scripture above:

Word(s) that come alive for me from this scripture:

What is God saying to me through these words?

🎧 **SONG FOR YOU**   MOST BEAUTIFUL / SO IN LOVE BY MAVERICK CITY MUSIC

Rest is a Place You Live

WEEK FIVE | 71

Day 2

What I tell them.

Who have you been listening to? You could be listening to you. An unrenewed version of you that tells you who you are not...a you that reminds you of mistakes you've made or a you that questions your qualification for what God has called you to. God has told you something that He intends for you to trust and follow. It only becomes difficult to follow God's word when we allow other voices to become an option.

Eve did not have an option other than to do what God told her until she allowed the enemy's voice to convince her that what God said wasn't true. She trusted God's word until she heard another word. What seemed good became an option. "There is a way that seems right to a man, but its end is the way of death." Proverbs 14:12 (NJKV). Whatever God has told you, trust that it will always be true and lead to what's best for you!

As I write to you now, I hear the Holy Spirit saying, *"If my children would do **what I tell them**, they would experience my rest and love on a deeper level they've never been before."* God wants to take you deeper in Him, to a place that is secure even when everything around you is falling apart. This is a real place, and He wants you to live there, but you must silence all other options and lean into His voice. The voice of feeling inadequate is no longer an option. The voice of what people think of you is no longer an option. The voice of your own will is not an option. "Trust in the Lord with all your heart, and lean not on your own understanding; in all your ways acknowledge Him, and He shall direct your paths. Do not be wise in your own eyes; Fear the Lord and depart from evil."

Proverbs 3:5-7 (NKJV). I believe there is a way to live by trusting God's voice, and its end is the way of rest.

Rest (menuwchah): Comfortable

Rest is a Place You Live

Day 2

My Hiding Place

> "For forty years I was angry with them, and I said,
> 'They are a people whose hearts
> turn away from me. They refuse to do what I tell them.'
> So in my anger I took an oath: 'They will never enter my place of rest.'"
>
> **PSALMS 95:10-11 (NLT)**

Write the scripture above:

Word(s) that come alive for me from this scripture:

What is God saying to me through these words?

🎧 **SONG FOR YOU**   DEEPER BY MARVIN SAPP

Rest is a Place You Live

Day 3

Hearts turn away.

To turn away is to reject or dismiss. When I see these words, I see a person turning their back away from their spouse or lover. Instead of talking it out, they close up and shut down, deciding not to trust their heart with the other. Rejecting someone/something can give us a false sense of protection when really, we are afraid to go to a place of true vulnerability. This place may have once been stung with disappointment or hurt from others, even as far back as a child. And so, we have conditioned our hearts to live in a place right outside of these walls. When a person or situation brings us near these fragile walls, we can become easily defensive, angered, guarded, or isolated. It feels easier to reject and dismiss than it is to enter this place we have so long kept protected. God wants you to enter this place again with Him and give you rest there. He doesn't want you to guard your heart from Him because of what others have done.

I remember praying one morning and telling God I want what He wants for me, and if it's His will for me to be married again, then I want that too. The Holy Spirit then said to me, *"But what do you want?"* God was taking me near a wall of a place I had guarded for so long. In the past, expressing my desires to a man resulted in rejection. Believing I was "guarding my heart," I had conditioned my ***heart to turn away*** from possible disappointment by not voicing my desires. I lived in a place where my life was more about pleasing others, even at the expense of my own comfort.

It's sad how we can pay the cost of comfortability to be at rest with others and yet be ok with the war within ourselves. After much thought, I opened up the door to that place and confessed, "I want to be married again." God then affirmed me that He is not like the other men in my past and that He can't lie. He promised not to leave me and that what I desired was because He first desired it for me.

Take an honest moment to meditate on where you have been living. Have you been living in a restless place with barbed wire around your heart? You can trust God to enter this place with you. He is not that person who left you abandoned or took advantage of you. He is the lover of your soul and a Father who beckons to talk it out with you. Turn your back around, look God in the face with your heart, and open up.

Rest (menuwchah): A resting place

Rest is a Place You Live

Day 3

My Hiding Place

"For forty years I was angry with them, and I said,
'They are a people whose hearts
turn away from me. They refuse to do what I tell them.'
So in my anger I took an oath: 'They will never enter my place of rest.'"

PSALMS 95:10-11 (NLT)

Write the scripture above:

Word(s) that come alive for me from this scripture:

What is God saying to me through these words?

🎧 **SONG FOR YOU** — OPEN MY HEART BY YOLANDA ADAMS

Rest is a Place You Live

Day 4

Enter.
Dear Child,
The door is unlocked to my place of rest
A home of quietness for your soul
A place for you to live, not as a guest
You only need to knock with a heart bent to my voice
For the posture of your heart gives access to ***enter***
So even with my invite, it'll always be your choice
Come in child from the pressures of life, from all of the stress
I can hear the cry of your soul
Tired and longing for my place of rest
Know that I want you here...here in this still place
Where you learn not to be easily moved
But to remain on shaky waters, focused on my face
Enter *this place of ease, where I am close, and anxiety is absent*
Where you are most alive, naked and unashamed
For your real home is in Me...you have my last name

Love,
~Your Father

Rest (menuwchah): Quietness, Ease, Still

Rest is a Place You Live

Day 4

My Hiding Place

"For forty years I was angry with them, and I said,
'They are a people whose hearts
turn away from me. They refuse to do what I tell them.'
So in my anger I took an oath: 'They will never enter my place of rest.'"

PSALMS 95:10-11 (NLT)

Write the scripture above:

Word(s) that come alive for me from this scripture:

What is God saying to me through these words?

🎧 SONG FOR YOU — COMMUNION BY MAVERICK CITY MUSIC

Rest is a Place You Live

Day 5

They are a people whose hearts.

Sometimes we can get so caught up in our financial, social, and career statuses that we put what matters most to God at the bottom - our heart status. God wants you to be financially successful. He wants you to have friends and enjoy social platforms. He wants you to operate in all the giftings and skills He embedded in you for your career. But God first wants your heart healthy so that everything you do is healthy. "Above all else, guard your heart, for everything you do flows from it." Proverbs 4:23 (NIV).

A person rich in money but poor in heart will use his money poorly. A person can have a large following, but if the heart has validation issues, they will use their platform for attention and likes. But a heart at rest in God can be used mightily by Him with their finances, on their YouTube channel, and in their career. He sees past all of the stuff we have on the outside of us and looks at our heart condition. "But the Lord said to Samuel, 'Do not look at his appearance or at his physical stature, because I have refused him. For the Lord does not see as man sees; for the man looks at the outward appearance, but the Lord looks at the heart.'" 1 Samuel 16:7 (NKJV).

Your heart matters to God because it is the room in your soul that motivates why you do what you do. God is looking for ***a people whose hearts*** are purely after His heart. For people who will respond to His call and not leave in the middle. When we find a resting place in Him, there is nowhere else our hearts will want to be. We will be ***a people whose hearts*** are for Him only. We will respond to the call and align with the promises that are on our life. Know that God knows your heart better than you! Lay before Him and ask what's in your heart that you may have looked passed. He wants your heart pure because a pure heart can be trusted. Spend more time on your heart status, and everything you do will flow from it.

Rest (menuwchah): A resting place

Rest is a Place You Live

Day 5

My Hiding Place

> "For forty years I was angry with them, and I said, 'They are a people whose hearts turn away from me. They refuse to do what I tell them.' So in my anger I took an oath: 'They will never enter my place of rest.'"
>
> **PSALMS 95:10-11 (NLT)**

Write the scripture above:

Word(s) that come alive for me from this scripture:

What is God saying to me through these words?

🎧 **SONG FOR YOU**   RESPOND BY TRAVIS GREENE

Rest is a Place You Live

Verse for the Weekend:

"When Jesus woke up, he rebuked the wind and said to the waves, "Silence! Be still!" Suddenly the wind stopped, and there was a great calm."

MARK 4:39 (NLT)

What stood out to me in the above verse?

Where does my heart find ease in a storm and in great calm?

Why should my heart face the Lord and not just my words?

REST
IN HIS
PROMISES

Week Six

Day 1

God is.

Growing up as the oldest of five siblings, I don't ever remember hearing my father tell any of us, "I promise." We knew when our father said something that is what it was or what it would be. I distinctly remember the time our parents surprised us with a trip to Universal Studios. When our father said we were going, we were shocked and excited because we'd never been, but we didn't doubt we were going because we knew our father.

Do you know your Heavenly Father? Do you know Him enough not to doubt the new places He's going to take you even though you've never been or seen it before? God wants His children to know Him, so that even when storms arise and panic starts to set in, we hold on to who we know Him to be and not what we see or don't see in the moment. **God is** our anchor! We can rest in His promises because we find rest in Him. His word is full of promises and who He is. **God is** a provider! "And my God shall supply all your need according to His riches in glory by Christ Jesus." Philippians 4:19 (NKJV). **God is** our strength! "The Lord is my strength and my shield; My heart trusted in Him, and I am helped; Therefore, my heart greatly rejoices, And with my song I will praise Him." Psalm 28:7 (NKJV).

Seek to know God for yourself by searching the word for His promises and who He is. Write them down, speak them aloud, and allow Him to show you over and over again that He is your anchor, your provider, and your strength! In this last week, we will meditate on a scripture that tells us who **God is** and what He promises us.

My prayer is that you see who you are as this word comes alive and that you find rest in Him and His promises!

> *"Christ is our Sabbath--we find rest in Him--not a day, but a person!"*
> *~ Creflo Dollar, American Televangelist*

Rest in His Promises

Day 1

My Hiding Place

> "God is our refuge and strength,
> always ready to help in times of trouble.
> So we will not fear when earthquakes come and the
> mountains crumble into the sea."
>
> **PSALMS 46:1-2 (NLT)**

Personalize the scripture above: (i.e. God is MY refuge...)

....
....
....
....

Word(s) that come alive for me from this scripture:

....
....

What is God saying to me through these words?

....
....
....

🎧 **SONG FOR YOU**   HAVEN'T SEEN IT YET BY DANNY GOKEY

Rest in His Promises

Day 2

Always ready to help.

Always is one of those words that gets tossed around lightly. I even find myself using it loosely when I tell a friend, "Whenever you need me, I'm always here." While our intentions may be in the right place, no one can make a promise that they will *always* be there. But God can, and He will! His word promises He's **always ready to help!**

God is not only always there, but He is ready! To be ready is to be in a suitable state for an activity, action, or situation; to be fully prepared, easily available, or within reach. We serve a God that is always in the perfect state for our situation. There is nothing you can go through or have done that God is not built to handle. He is fully prepared to help you in the troubles of your marriage, your finances, your kids, your job, or discovering your purpose! I love that to be ready also means to be easily available or within reach.

As a kid, I used to believe that God only spoke to the pastors and all those who sat in the pulpit. I thought that God called them to a position that had a "special connection" with Him. I never knew that God was within my reach, even as a kid. To the one who feels unworthy of His love, He's within reach! To the other that wants to hear His voice and never had, He's within reach! To another whose lost hope and with it lost their relationship with the Father, He's still within reach!

God is **always ready to help**, now are you ready to receive it? See, true rest doesn't come just because you know who the word says God is, but it is also when you receive who you are because of who He is! Since He is **always ready to help you,** you are never in a place you can't be helped. You are never in a place that is too far or hard for Him. "Dear friends, if we don't feel guilty, we can come to God with bold confidence." 1 John 3:21 (NLT). Don't allow your feelings to stop you from coming to God for help. You can come boldly before your Father because you are His child, and that is what children do. When you call for His help, rest in knowing He hears you. He's available and suitable to help you!

> *"Rest is a place you are untouchable because you know who God says you are!"* ~ Unknown

Rest in His Promises

Day 2

My Hiding Place

> "God is our refuge and strength,
> always ready to help in times of trouble.
> So we will not fear when earthquakes come and the
> mountains crumble into the sea."
>
> **PSALMS 46:1-2 (NLT)**

Personalize the scripture above: (i.e. God is MY refuge...)

....

....

....

....

Word(s) that come alive for me from this scripture:

....

....

What is God saying to me through these words?

....

....

....

🎧 **SONG FOR YOU**   REAL THING BY MAVERICK CITY MUSIC

Rest in His Promises

Day 3

Will not fear.

I am currently in the process of working on my will so that my family knows what I wish for them to have after I pass away. I didn't realize how important this was to have until I heard horrible stories of siblings fighting and getting lawyers. Oh no! Even if I'm gone, the thought of the ruin that could come to my family because I didn't put my will into place beforehand bothers me.

We put off things like this because either we think we're too young to have a will, don't know the importance of a will, or don't want to think about the inevitable - death. Just as we all will pass away; we all will face trouble and hard times at some point in our lives. Let's put our will into place now by making up in our minds ***we will not fear!*** Draw the line in the dirt, root your feet, and hold your stance here! Behind this line is no fear, no worry, and no stress. This is where we will stand!

The sons of Korah were imagining the worst that could happen to them when they sang in Psalms 46 of earthquakes coming and mountains crumbling. Yet they were able to make this powerful declaration because they knew if they entrusted themselves to God, they had no reason to fear. When we fear, stress or worry, it is because we are carrying the responsibility of God. When we rest and trust God, we remain in position for Him to fight our battles and for His promises to manifest in our lives! So if you have not started, begin the process of intentionally working on your ***will not to fear***.

"You can't receive the promise out of worry or stress. When you rest is when it manifests!" ~ *Creflo Dollar*

Rest in His Promises

Day 3

My Hiding Place

> "God is our refuge and strength,
> always ready to help in times of trouble.
> So we will not fear when earthquakes come and the
> mountains crumble into the sea."

PSALMS 46:1-2 (NLT)

Personalize the scripture above: (i.e. God is MY refuge...)

....

....

....

....

Word(s) that come alive for me from this scripture:

....

....

What is God saying to me through these words?

....

....

....

🎧 **SONG FOR YOU** I WILL TRUST BY FRED HAMMOND

Rest in His Promises

Day 4

Crumble.

To crumble is to break or fall apart, to be greatly shaken. Have you ever seen a mountain crumble? Me neither. But the very thing that looks to be unbreakable, that can withstand great disturbance, can **crumble.**

We do such a great job in masking our insecurities and deep-rooted issues until an earthquake shakes us at the core. And for some, it doesn't take much more than a wrong look to break you. The more you deal with the core of who you are, the more humility you will have in how you present yourself to people and *earthquakes*. You come to realize that it is only God you can be confident in and not your fragile self. This is why Psalms 46 begins with who God is. God is secure! He can't **crumble.** We have living within us the God that can't crumble! "We now have this light shining in our hearts, but we ourselves are like fragile clay jars containing this great treasure. This makes it clear that our great power is from God, not from ourselves." 2 Corinthians 4:7 (NLT).

Take it from a woman whose life was plagued with insecurity since she was a young girl. She was afraid to speak up for herself and eased her pain by escaping in her own written fantasy stories. She didn't know who she was because she covered it for so long in fear of rejection. Now this woman has a heart for God's people, prays for the broken, is using her gift of writing to build God's people, and walks confidently because her confidence is in God! I am no longer bound to insecurity, but I am free because I have learned to rest in the one who does not **crumble!**

"Being at rest is to remain confident, free from anxiety or disturbance." ~ Tony Peterson, Senior Pastor

Rest in His Promises

Day 4

My Hiding Place

> "God is our refuge and strength,
> always ready to help in times of trouble.
> So we will not fear when earthquakes come and the
> mountains crumble into the sea."
>
> **PSALMS 46:1-2 (NLT)**

Personalize the scripture above: (i.e. God is MY refuge...)

_____

_____

_____

_____

Word(s) that come alive for me from this scripture:

_____

_____

What is God saying to me through these words?

_____

_____

_____

🎧 **SONG FOR YOU**   NO BONDAGE BY JUBILEE WORSHIP

Rest in His Promises

Day 5

Refuge and strength.

Dear Child,

    *I see you. I see your fears. I see your strengths. I see what moves you. I see what causes the wonder in your eye. I hear your heart and the song of your soul. I know its desires and its tender places. Oh, if you knew how much my heart overwhelms with love for you, you would seek my **refuge and strength** daily. But you can know. I call you to know Me, to know my love, for I am Love. There's more to Me than just my hands. There's more to you than just your hands. Just as you were created to create, you were also created to rest. It's who you are. Will you seek to find rest in Me? To rest in Me is to love Me. To rest in Me is to know I am your Hiding Place. You can run in, and I am always there, protecting you and loving you as my word promises. You do not have to be afraid, for there is rest in the place you are in. There is **refuge and strength** for your soul.*

> *"Rest is not something you do; it's who you are, a place you are in." ~ Tony Peterson*

Rest in His Promises

Day 5

My Hiding Place

> "God is our refuge and strength,
> always ready to help in times of trouble.
> So we will not fear when earthquakes come and the
> mountains crumble into the sea."
>
> **PSALMS 46:1-2 (NLT)**

Personalize the scripture above: (i.e. God is MY refuge...)

....

....

....

....

Word(s) that come alive for me from this scripture:

....

....

What is God saying to me through these words?

....

....

🎧 **SONG FOR YOU**   MY SOUL SINGS BY MAVERICK CITY MUSIC

Rest in His Promises

Verse for the Weekend:

"Then he asked them, "Why are you afraid?
Do you still have no faith?"
The disciples were absolutely terrified. "Who is this man?"
they asked each other.
"Even the wind and waves obey him!"

MARK 4:40-41 (NLT)

What stood out to me in the above verse?

Who is God to me?

Why should I not be afraid when trouble arises?

Printed in Great Britain
by Amazon